Dear Parent:

Your child's love of reading starts here!

Every child learns to read in a different way and at his or her own speed. Some go back and forth between reading levels and read favourite books again and again. Others read through each level in order. You can help your young reader improve and become more confident by encouraging his or her own interests and abilities. From books your child reads with you to the first books he or she reads alone, there are I Can Read Books for every stage of reading:

SHARED READING
Basic language, word repetition, and whimsical illustrations, ideal for sharing with your emergent reader

BEGINNING READING
Short sentences, familiar words, and simple concepts for children eager to read on their own

READING WITH HELP
Engaging stories, longer sentences, and language play for developing readers

READING ALONE
Complex plots, challenging vocabulary, and high-interest topics for the independent reader

I Can Read Books have introduced children to the joy of reading since 1957. Featuring award-winning authors and illustrators and a fabulous cast of beloved characters, I Can Read Books set the standard for beginning readers.

A lifetime of discovery begins with the magical words "I Can Read!"

Visit www.icanread.ca for information
on enriching your child's reading experience.

I Can Read Book® is a trademark of HarperCollins Publishers

Viola Desmond: A Hero for Us All
Text copyright © 2019 by HarperCollins Publishers Ltd.
Pictures © 2019 by Nick Craine.
All rights reserved. Published by Collins, an imprint of HarperCollins Publishers Ltd.

This work is adapted from "Viola Desmond Takes Her Seat" in *5-Minute Stories for Fearless Girls* by Sarah Howden,
illustrations by Nick Craine.

Images of the $10 bank note reproduced with the permission of the Bank of Canada.

HarperCollins books may be purchased for educational, business, or sales promotional use through our Special Markets Department.

HarperCollins Publishers Ltd
Bay Adelaide Centre, East Tower
22 Adelaide Street West, 41st Floor
Toronto, Ontario, Canada
M5H 4E3

www.harpercollins.ca

Library and Archives Canada Cataloguing in Publication information is available upon request.

www.icanread.ca

ISBN 978-1-4434-5983-9

WZL 1 2 3 4 5 6 7 8 9 10

VIOLA DESMOND:
A HERO FOR US ALL

by Sarah Howden
pictures by Nick Craine

Collins

It was my birthday.

I opened my card from Grandma.

Inside was a ten-dollar bill!

"Thank you!" I said.

I gave her a hug.

"And look who's on it," she said.

It was a smiling lady.

She looked kind.

"That's Viola Desmond,"

my grandma said.

"Who's that?" I asked.

Grandma looked surprised.

"Let me tell you a story," she said.

One day Viola Desmond was driving.

She was on her way

to Sydney, Nova Scotia.

It was 1946.

But all of a sudden

her car made a noise.

Clunk, clunk, BANG.

Viola found a garage.

"Your car needs a new part,"

the mechanic told her.

The car wouldn't be ready
until the next day.
"Oh dear," said Viola.

But then Viola shrugged.

"I'll get a hotel room," she said.

"I'll make the best of it."

Viola didn't have a free
night very often.
"I'll go to the movies,"
she said with a smile.

13

The theatre was called the Roseland.

"One ticket, please," said Viola
at the booth.

"I'd like a downstairs seat."

The downstairs tickets cost more.

But they were worth it for the view.

Viola got her ticket.

She went in and sat down.

Then she felt a tap on her shoulder.

"I think you have a balcony seat,"

the usher said.

Viola took out her ticket.

The usher was right.

Her ticket said BALCONY.

Viola went back to the booth.

"Can I have a downstairs ticket instead?" Viola asked.

The clerk looked at her.

"We don't sell downstairs tickets to you people," the clerk said. Now Viola understood.

It was because she was black.

The theatre had a racist rule.

Only white people could sit

downstairs.

Viola wanted to cry.

But she took a deep breath

and stood up straight.

"It isn't fair," Viola said.

So Viola walked back inside.

And she sat downstairs.

"You need to move,"

the manager said.

But Viola stayed put.

"I paid for my ticket," she said.

"I just want to watch the movie."

The manager's face turned red.

He stomped off.

He came back with a police officer.

"You need to sit upstairs,"
said the officer.

"No, thank you," said Viola.

"Then you will have to come with me," the officer said.

He took Viola to jail.

She had to stay there overnight.

The next day Viola was sent home.

All she wanted was to rest.

But she knew she had more to do.

Viola gathered all her friends.

Viola told them what had happened.

"Black people are equal," she said.

"We deserve better."

The word began to spread.

Viola had taken a stand.

Now others felt like they could too.

"Viola spoke up for equality,"
Grandma said.

"She was very brave.
And slowly change did come."

I looked down at my ten-dollar bill.
"I want to keep this
someplace special," I said.
"So I can remember to be brave,
just like Viola."